UNITED STATES

Written by Doug Barone

COUNTRIES of the WORLD

I0801636

PowerKiDS press

Published in 2025
by The Rosen Publishing Group, Inc.
2544 Clinton Street, Buffalo, NY 14224

© 2024 BookLife Publishing Ltd.

Written by: Doug Barone
Edited by: Elise Carraway
Designed by: Miranda Tremere

Cataloging-in-Publication Data

Names: Barone, Doug.
Title: United States / Doug Barone.
Description: Buffalo, NY : PowerKids Press, 2025. | Series: Countries of the world | Includes glossary and index.
Identifiers: ISBN 9781499447330 (pbk.) | ISBN 9781499447347 (library bound) | ISBN 9781499447354 (ebook)
Subjects: LCSH: United States--Juvenile literature.
Classification: LCC E178.3 B376 2025 | DDC 973--dc23

All rights reserved.

No part of this book may be reproduced in any form without permission in writing from the publisher, except by a reviewer.

Manufactured in the United States of America
CPSIA Compliance Information: Batch #CSPK25. For further information contact Rosen Publishing at 1-800-237-9932.

Find us on

Image Credits
All images are courtesy of Shutterstock.com, unless otherwise specified. With thanks to Getty Images, Thinkstock Photo and iStockphoto. Cover – critterbiz, FloridaStock, TTstudio, Anna Kosheleva, GoodStudio. 2 – Galyna Andrushko. 4–5 – Andrew Minsk, Lucky-photographer. 6–7 – Huntstyle, Big Bear Aerials. 8–9 – Tijana Moraca, FamVeld. 10–11 – Ground Picture, LightField Studios. 12–13 – FamVeld, Monkey Business Images. 14–15 – solepsizm, Konstantin L. 16–17 – SOK Studio, Roman Samborskyi. 18–19 – JoeSAPhotos, Steve Broer. 20–21 – JeniFoto, Sean Locke Photography. 22–23 – sherwood, NASA, Public domain, via Wikimedia Commons.

CONTENTS

Words that look like this can be found in the glossary on page 24.

WHERE IS THE UNITED STATES OF AMERICA?

The United States of America is a country in North America. It is made up of 50 areas called states.

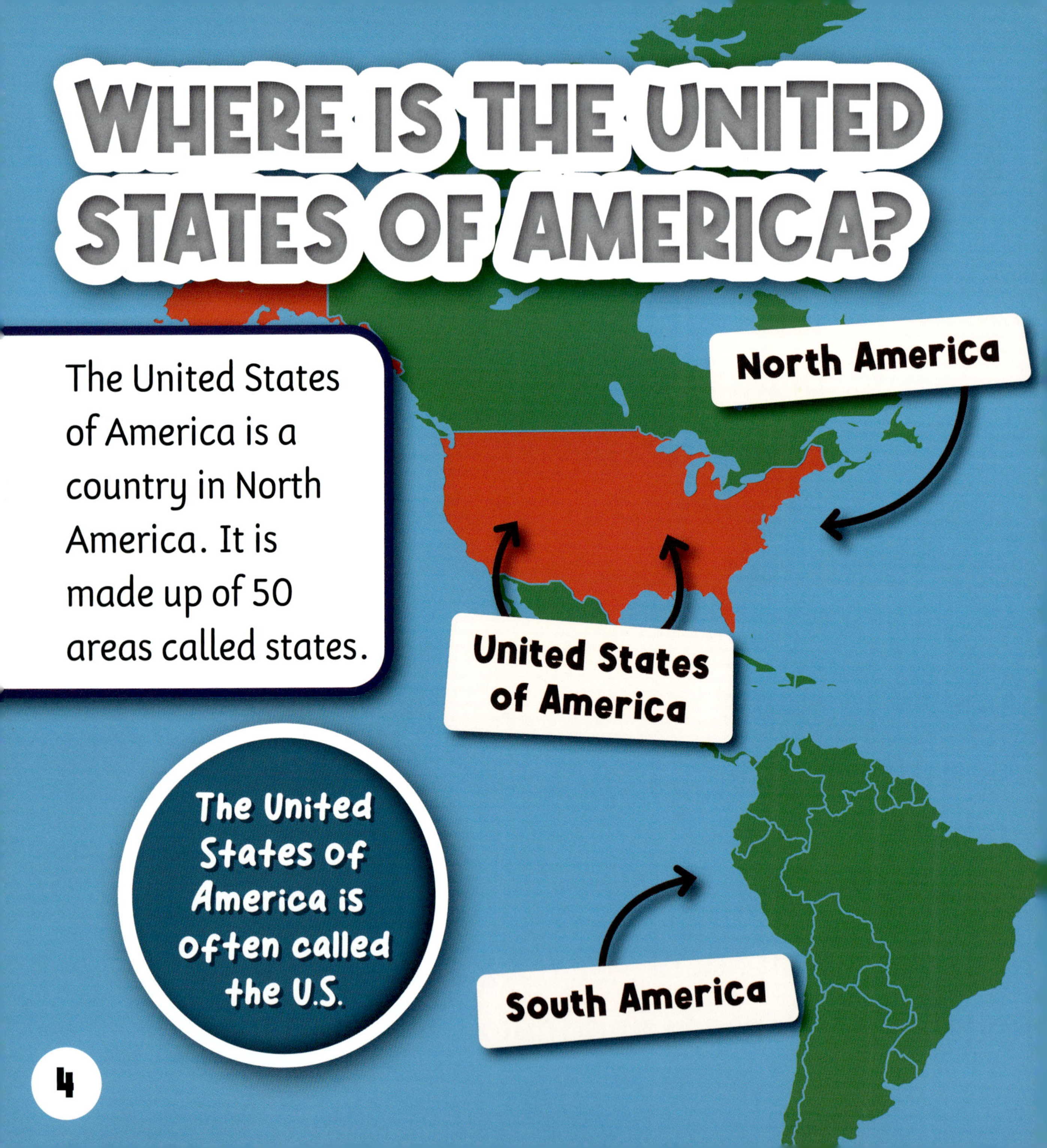

The United States of America is often called the U.S.

Millions of people in the U.S. live in large cities, such as Los Angeles and New York City. The most spoken language in the U.S. is English.

Washington, D.C., is the capital of the U.S.

Washington, D.C.

LANDSCAPE AND WEATHER

The weather in the U.S. is different in different parts of the country. Some places get tornadoes and other kinds of extreme weather quite often.

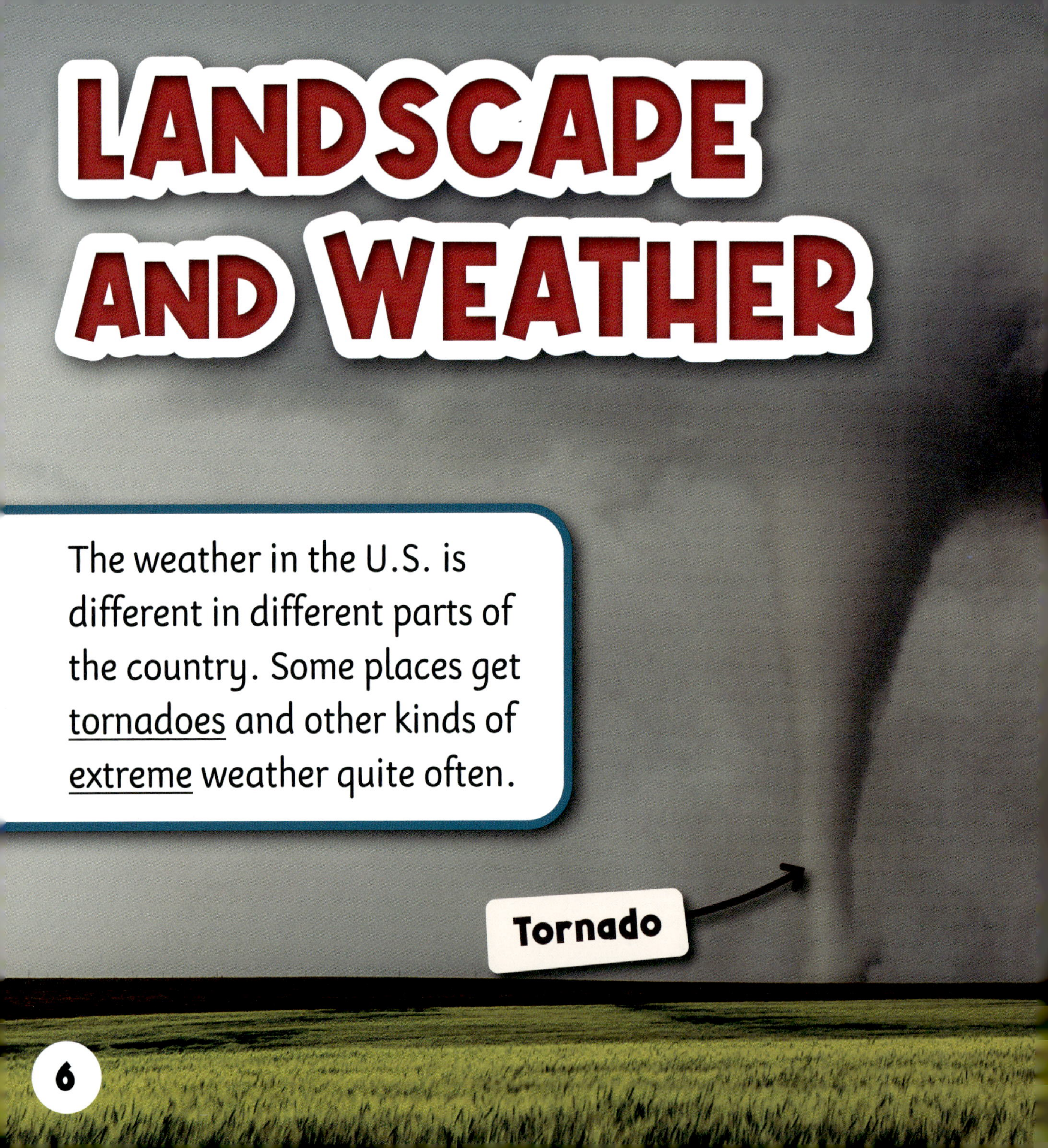

There are many different types of landscapes in the U.S. There are mountains, forests, and rivers.

The Missouri River is the longest river in the U.S.

RELIGION

The religion with the most followers in the U.S. is Christianity. Christians celebrate special events throughout the year, such as Christmas and Easter.

There are also people in the U.S. who follow other religions, such as Judaism, Islam, and Hinduism.

FAMILIES

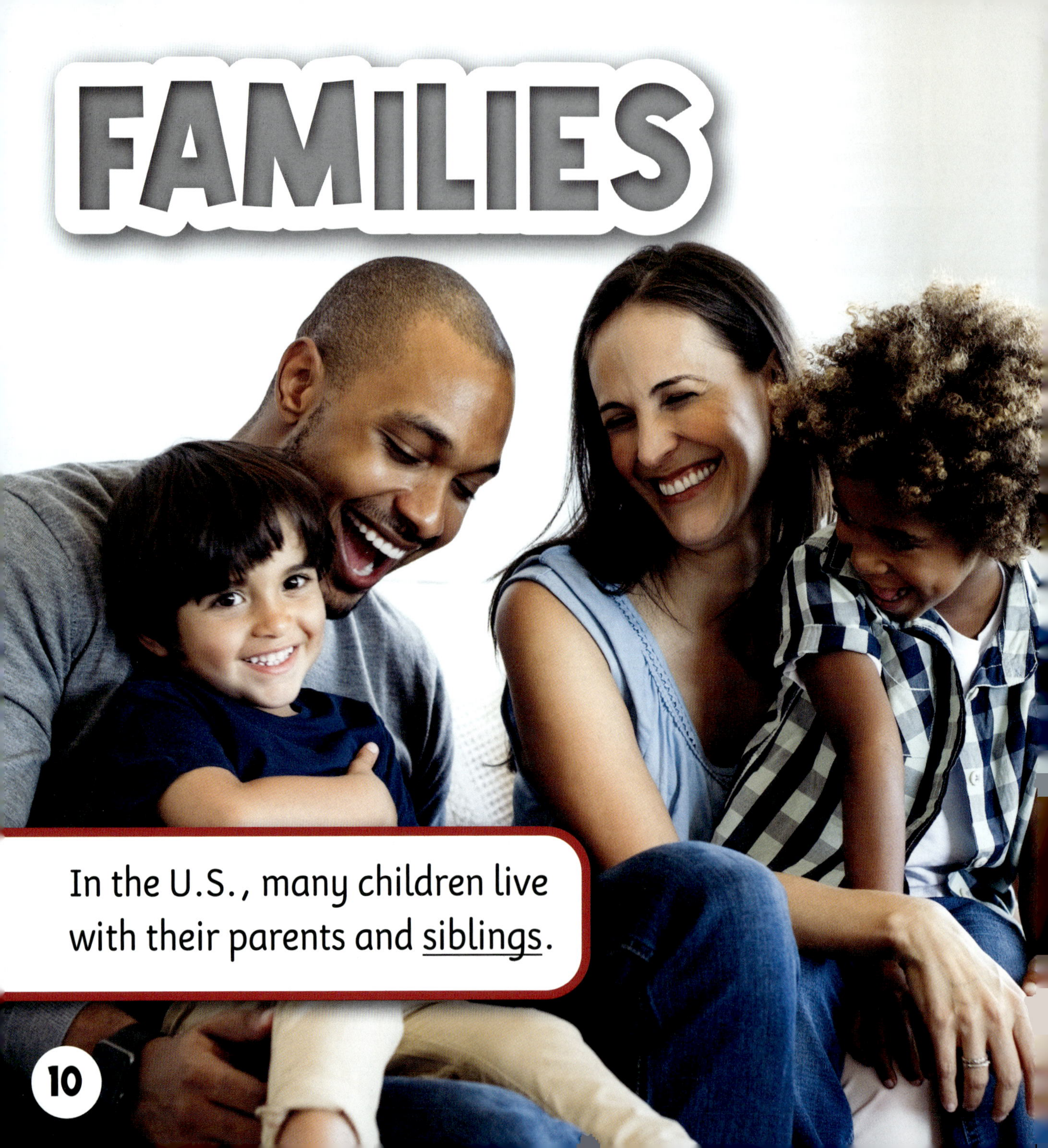

In the U.S., many children live with their parents and siblings.

Many families in the U.S. like to get together to celebrate special occasions, such as Thanksgiving.

SCHOOL

Children starting school in the U.S. usually go to kindergarten in their first year. In kindergarten, children learn how to draw, read, and write.

After the first year in kindergarten, children move through school grades each year, from first grade to twelfth grade.

HOME

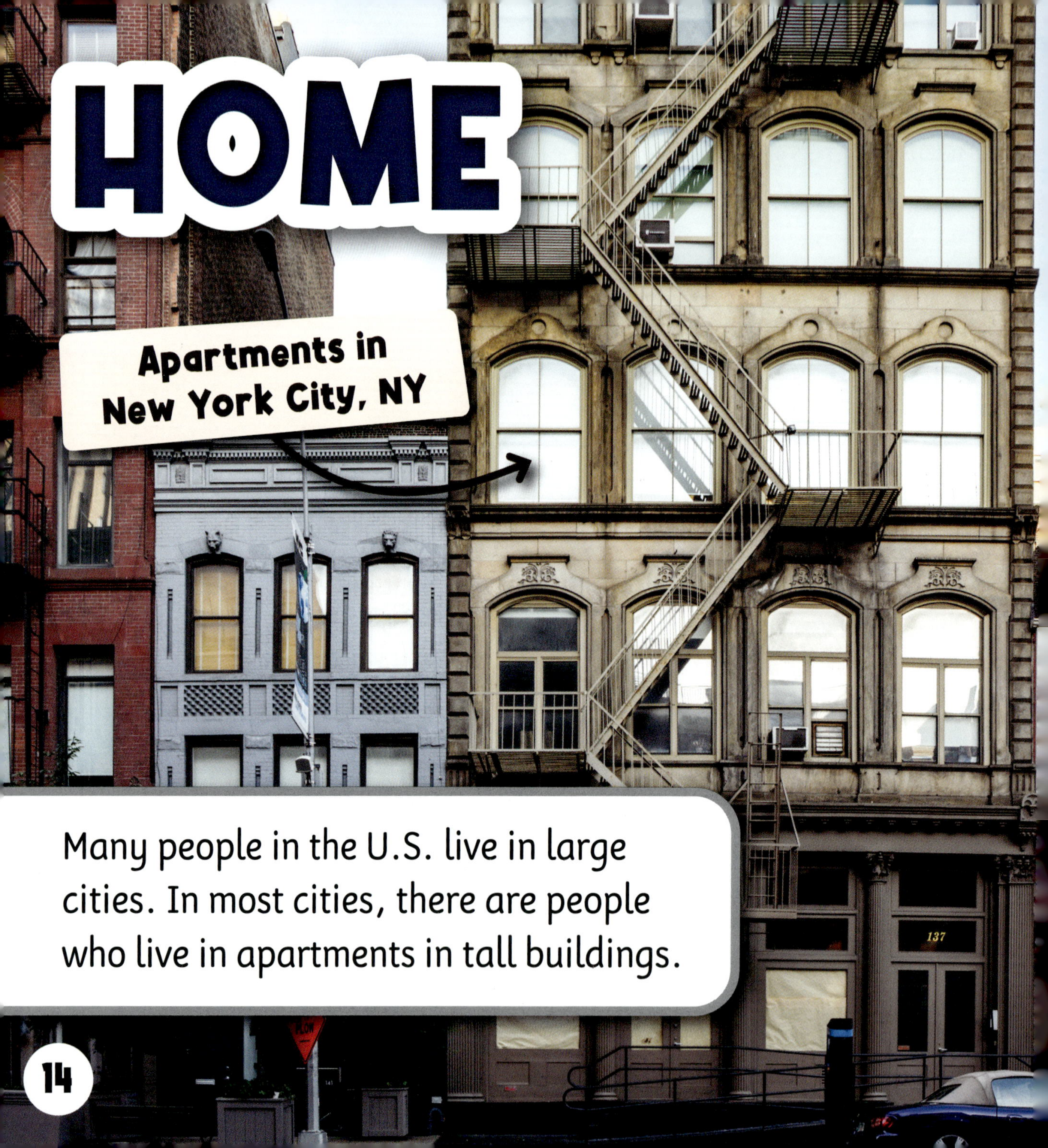

Apartments in New York City, NY

Many people in the U.S. live in large cities. In most cities, there are people who live in apartments in tall buildings.

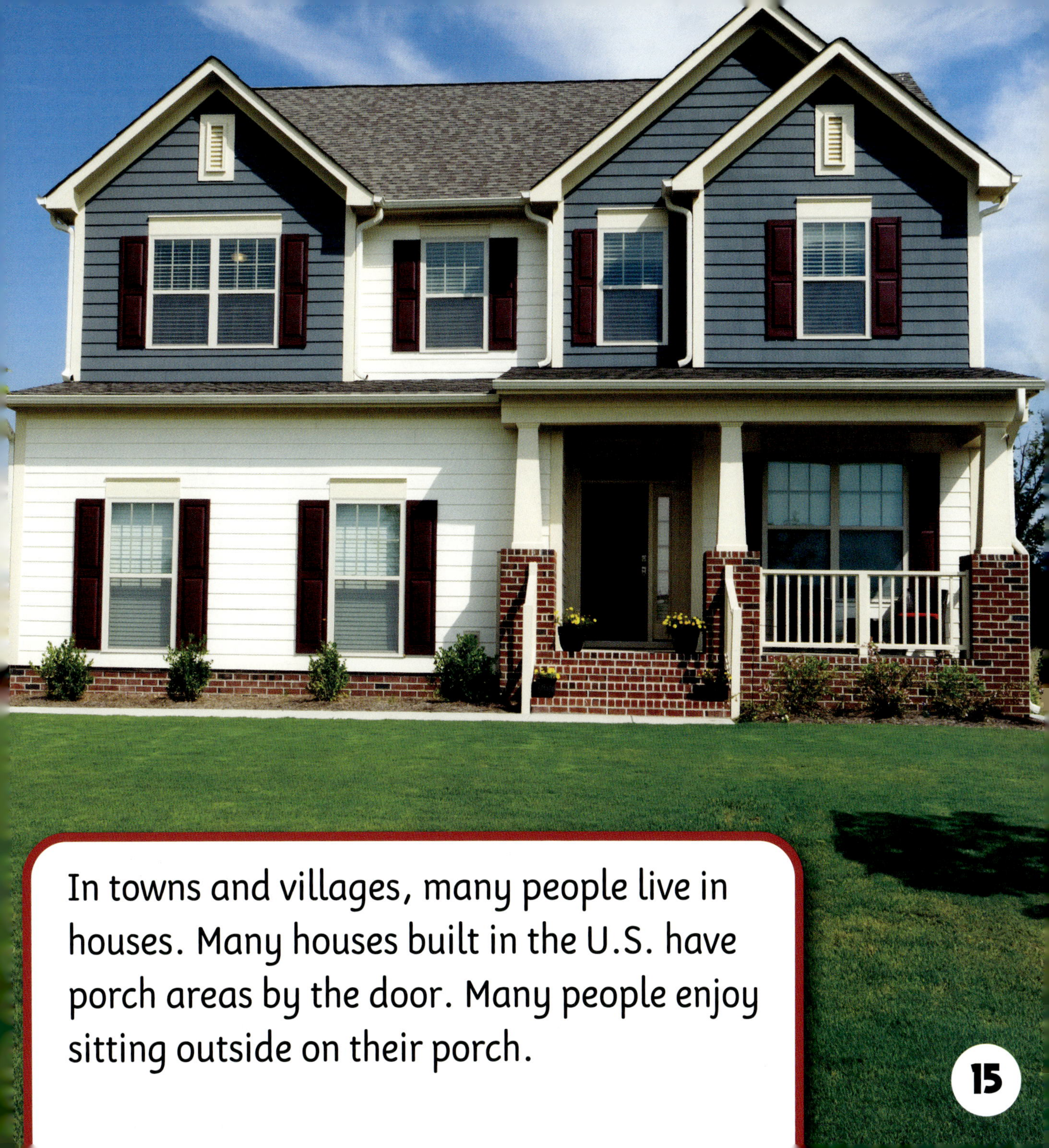

In towns and villages, many people live in houses. Many houses built in the U.S. have porch areas by the door. Many people enjoy sitting outside on their porch.

CLOTHING

Many people living in the U.S. dress in comfortable clothing, such as jeans and a T-shirt.

Blue jeans are very popular in the U.S. They are made from a material called denim.

SPORTS

People in the U.S. are known for enjoying many different types of sports. One of the most popular sports is American football.

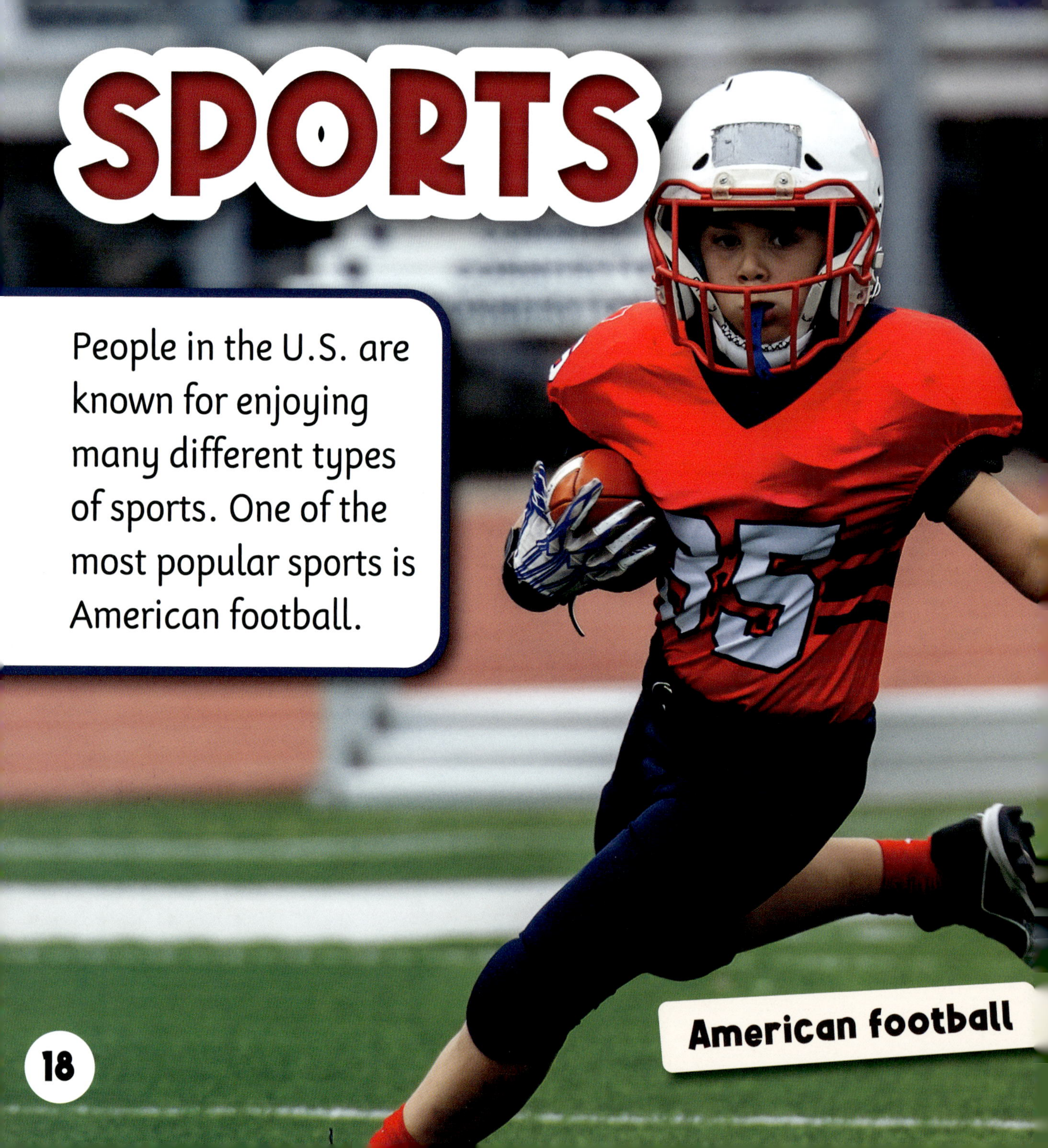

American football

Every year, a huge game of American football takes place in the U.S. It is called the Super Bowl. Thousands of people go to watch it in person.

FOOD

Apple pie is a popular dish in the U.S. It is made from baked apples and pastry.

Hot dogs are also very popular in the U.S. A hot dog is a cooked sausage in a sliced bun.

Neil Armstrong was an astronaut from the United States. He was the first person to walk on the moon.

He said, "That's one small step for man, one giant leap for mankind."

There are cowboys and cowgirls living and working in some parts of the U.S. They wear special boots and hats and often spend their day riding horses and looking after cows.

GLOSSARY

astronaut someone who is trained to go up into space

extreme dangerous and serious

kindergarten the first year of formal school in the United States

material fabric or cloth

religion a system of faith and worship, especially to do with a god or gods

siblings brothers and sisters

Thanksgiving a national holiday in the United States

tornadoes fast-moving, strong winds that form into funnel shapes

INDEX